"A Second life in Virtual Worlds."

ISBN 978-1-4348-3722-6

Printed in the Untied States

Copyright 2008 © Dale Calhoun\Mcgee

True to the Vine International.

Contents

1. Introduction.

2. The internet is mass archive.

3. The *If* Condition.

4. 9111.

5. Games in Second life.

6. Rediscovering yourself.

7. More about Baby-boomers.

8. Mental health on the web.

9. The Other identity theft.

10. The New Matrix.

11. Concluding remarks.

12. Stories of the Computer.

13. Your Personal Journal.

14. Glossary of Terms.

15. Computer Lexicon.

16. Hackers Glossary.

17. Authors Glossary.

18. Computer Addiction Test.

19. Order out Chaos.

20. Appendix.

About the Author;

The Author has been on the internet from 1996 sense his accident in December 19, 1995 in Dexter Missouri working for Hudson Foods. He has taken several courses dealing with the Graphic Arts, and Computer science and being a Internet Specialist. He is a graduate of US Armys exstensive electronics training at Redstone arsenal of Restone Alabama for a former Missile system that's has been upgraded and renamed. He has had 12 years security experiance in various security positions dealing with military and cilivian jobs. Including Computer and security camera monitoring and patrol manager. He has been a sales representive for a Seattle Base Company for 5 years. He is a self styled entrepreneur selling books, and e-books on his internet web-site and LULU.com.

Introductions from the top:

As usual all my books are a work in progress and I have many additions to the main theme of the book. As an example of virtual worlds this book deals with gaming in Secondlife.com from the banning of gambling.

I have been in many chat rooms, and virtual spaces.

I find a lot more flexibility in secondlife.com to do commerce.

I have had enough of all the chatter and the mind games of fantasy with the internet.

I'am strictly a business man when it comes to the internet.

I sell on e-bay and write books and will get into more script writing in the future and write my notes in this book.

At the end of this book deals a lot with internet recovery and support groups. This is what we will have to deal with in the future as technologie advances. While a lot of what is presented in this book are predictions, humor, opinions, the author knows the computer age changes rapidly and so will any theory presented here. It could be larger then life or smaller then the eye of the neetle. Perhaps, before its time if its renderings carrie a message of hope for generations to come. Either way some issues are coming to light rapidly before this book is even finished watch your news casts.

The addictions to internet life which is really no life to exist in alone. We should start early with support groups helping people overcome their problems with interversions because of the internet. In some cases it might even seem hypercritical to deal with some areas like casinos on the internet. This reality must be addressed because in the USA its illegal. If your addicted to it then its possible its something you need to elminate and address for the healing to begin. Second Life no longer has gambling for now. This will be addressed later in chapters to come.

Yes, it is suggested in some cases intervention and deprogramming should be done in order for any real healing to begin. This book is written for the average person to understand without all the mathicmatics just simple lay terms in plain english. Even this can be easy to get lost within a subject until you experience scripting, perhaps Html, and hooked on java program writing. These to me are the easyiest beginnings of learning about how a web site is constructed. Read books like Html publishing Bible by Alan Simpson. Yes you can be self taught you don't have to have expensive College Courses to learn the computer. Even though it looks good on your resume with this experience.

If you ever get your foot in the door for a data entry job this is a great start for bigger and larger prospects with Technologies or a Computer degree perhaps with only a 2 year college degree. It depends how far up the corperate later you want to go with your career in computers. Gameing programming takes many hours of your time locked in spaces figuring the next phaze of the game you are to incorperate.I never went that far because I'am not patient enough to live in such a closed envirnment figuring these things out. I have written small internet programs but always modelled them after another program I found off the internet along with some tweaks here and there. Never got any money for my work but most of my studies are dedicated to my research into the field. As most of my readers will know most of my books when dealing with PEER groups are centered around the hypothesis that most human beings have an addictive spirit. Its not just sexual, or drug addictions, it can be for food, for the love money even relgious in nature. I try to encorperate solutions for groups of people to be able help each other through some base PEER group interactions. It has been proven from time to time that these group member situations have helped 75% or more people these figures depends on the group. The 25% lesser amount it hasn't helped perhaps because of some kinda of block in personality related to envirmental issues. I will write my observances until I find the right avenue for that persons need for true social interaction to begin. If you start a PEER group make it unique to your members not like any other.

The internet is an mass archive

of information world wide. You have left to right wing ideas. Just do a internet search and you'll find every site there is and groups that believe the same way you do. Hopefully for the good not How to construct a bomb. How be a terrorist. How to steal identity.

The fast pace world clearly is in the internet. The desire to control it; is the concern of nations. Some people don't have the rights to surf like we do as a free nation and our Net-Neutrality. Because world leaders know its a powerful tool to spread

In this book we are exploring both predictions and research into the future technology of the computer. In the back of this book the author has included the social recovery some will have to go through in order to bring back the social balance they will need from returning from VR (Virtual Reality) worlds. This research is for future reference. Perhaps some issues are ahead of its time it will not be taken seriously in the beginning. Like science fiction without a story line but science fiction in many ways has been a self-fulfilling prophecy of mankind's destiny into the future of his existence. But in do time when VR worlds like Second Life take on AI traits then people will see the urgency for recovery both in ones personal life and ones work life. This book is not trying to be an alarmist reading with issues of end-times scenarios rather a researcher with predictions about Virtual worlds and mental health. Bringing out the why we need to get a handle on this now to build a better future. As long as scripted worlds are scripted they will always have a Borg typed collective. (Star Trek) Other then the UI being under the control of a User to make free decisions the actual objects will always be tied to each other. Within this book we will conduct several experiments for secondlife users to try this theory out. Secondlife has been the platform most of these experiments have been placed within this book. Because of the great UI (User Interface) which has Voice activation now.

Another awareness here is it has the best glossary of terms to work from to get an understanding of what we are talking about. Some scripts will be explored in this book but for the most part will be used to compare scripting programs for editing purposes. Its founder Philip Rosendale is a great example of a visionary of Virtual Worlds to be used for business and entertainment. Let it be added I base my opinions of my research and facts, as I understand them. I have not the qualifications to pass industry judgments based on my degree of intelligence. In fact predictions have a habit of being put down as fact until the test of time. It could be ten to twenty years before one actually comes to past. But that is why I included the chapter 9111 because it includes the cyber industry predictions of a great terrorist attack on us.

Another though not the complete manuscript to the future it talks about the back door into computer system built around UI technology. This I believe includes the if command as I included it in my next chapter.

It has been said the computers do not have a true random. I beg to differ when it's the user who computes the program to create random. Such as fortuneteller programs when a number randomly shows up. This is a task I achieved when I integrated a program from my Sinclair computer to Commodore computer using random program. Random will have to be the future for robotics if they are to make their own decisions without a user standing over them.

The If Condition

In computer language or scripting as it is called in Virtual worlds their still exists a command language in computer as in life that is the condition of **IF**. (See glossary of terms for all adverbs) this is a word that poses a question concerning a condition. That question is either true or false.

Interesting enough it is question poses to human beings through out history. John 8:31 "**If** you abide in my word, you are my disciples indeed. And you shall know the truth, and the truth shall make you free." Interesting enough again we find the self-fulfilling prophecy of scriptures if we read Eph 6:11 you will find the futuristic secret of overcoming technology it's the full armor of God and will be futuristic as well. We are to obey those who have authority over us in the same hand not with eye service as men pleasers but to do the will of God from the heart. I'm keying up on some of the most important words here as it fits into the computer age to come. We're to do our service as unto the Lord and not to man. The key here is not to let the eyes fixated to the Internet but to do service from the heart. The eyes are the windows of the soul therefore we're not to let the mind zombie out the condition is to listen to the heart not the fleshly ramblings of the wandering mind. You read the term wiles of the devil in the King James while this interprets to mean devices. Interesting enough there are devices for the good and evil on earth. The computer easily falls into that category by the hands of the user who operates the device. We read about term's lions to girt them up we sit in the seat with our lions also the feet planted I can't help but to see a figure of man sitting at a computer desk operating a computer. The shield is to guard our heart because it's the faith we are sharing the fiery darts come across the wire to the computer. Radiation from the computer screen and within parts of the computer devices we are shielded from many things that could cause great damage. I can go on and on of the coalition of the bible to modern times. These words of the bible are for future of mankind to interpret for his time. And now this word *If* courses through the wire of great computers in the world. Able to make lightening fast decisions. Interesting adverbs that conduct binary action on the computer software life like THEN and ELSE each a meaning in decision making like humankind. *IF* meets the condition for THEN to achieve its next move while ELSE resolves the decision as to wither it is the right choice. Followed by numbers and logic with in the program being executed. Interesting enough these adverbs it can be said through binary code equal cause and effect in human relativity.

I remember back in the early 1980's when this word was present in the evolution of the home lap top computer.

Apple, Commodore, Sinclair just to name a few If they didn't have if they had a substitute word to replace it but over all the word won out in common computer language and is with us still today.

You will find if in second life in it's scripting language. In the evolution of AI this will be an embedded word the many words in the conduct and actions of software inside the hardware cued to the headset of a user. Why hasn't this Lawnmower man technology been as popular in beginnings of the 21st century?

It's being perfected think of the eye problems if this isn't perfected and the lawsuits. I will have already pointed out in a chapter later of this and the many mental health problems we will face if the addiction to the computer isn't solved early in a users lifetime their could be long term results.

What does this mean? To stop using the computer completely? No, we need the positive influence on the Internet and operating the Computer. If there was a one-world take over we need the computer genius to help us hack into the system. The concern with is living the passing fantasy the endless rebounds of empty relationships.

Do to the exclusiveness in personality changes losing the social structure of a normal life. The term get a life is real because a computer screen doesn't put love vibrations in your soul.

Its wrong to justify entrapment on people in the crimes of passion do to the fantasy world of the Internet Many 13 year olds pose as adults online as a prank or to find meaning. Adults are sucked in daily by the fantasy world online. It's a mind game that should be stopped but not at expense of people's jobs it's like being mentally raped. It's a learning process to be unlearned from bad habits that have been introduced online. You can change your name how you look you can be bigger then you really are you can start business without licenses if a company sponsors you.

It's right to educate about the crimes and how avoid the pitfalls the Internet. We must stop the seasoned predator that stocks the information highway in all kinds of cloaks. We aren't talking about your convicted sex offender.

But the novice user that must be educated about what laws can be broken by playing hacker online like the kid who runs his parents phone bill up to $2000 not realizing he's been running a long distant phone bill up calling AOL's 1-800 number. Meanwhile when found out the bill is dismissed because of a misunderstanding and a kind of grace from the Telephone Company giving adults the benefit of the doubt for their children's lack of understanding.

There must be some kind of grace giving to a first time offense. For those not on probation for real-time crimes. A mental Re-hab of the sorts a group therapy and recovery back to a normal society. That is the whole of this book trying to help give some structure to a normal life while enjoying the computer but having a real social life outside the restraints of the pixels of the computer screen.

Let me conclude this chapter with the another bible coalition to the computer age to come. In Colossians 1: 16-17 it talks about Thrones, dominions, and principalities and powers saying "all things were created by him:" While I don't offer the theologian scholarship here I can offer you this for those who look to do right in ages to come. These are great times we are living as we see the unfolding of the banner of the Lord.

In my study of the word throne I found that its meaning stems to the term of many eyed ones. You know a throne is a seat in the word principality I read it means a person commencing or going forth powers always stems from the power of choice the passage of choice and liberty in doing what pleases. In other words permission granted. A term used in computers comes forth from the word of God next is Dominion the power of leadership possession. It says in Rev 19:16 he "had on his vest and on his thigh King of Kings and Lord of Lords." In the age to come I feel we'll see his glory by a great prediction in that day to gather where all will see his glory. There will be false interpretations and rumors of every kind but I do believe the confirmation will come by the age of technology as never seen before perhaps the window to usher him into the final age. I believe I may not live to see the fullness of this age. But I will see many hints and glances as I see now as the Kingdom advances from glory to glory and precept upon precept my prodigy will come to advance the work a true Godsend.

9111

This chapter is a brief outline of my book by the same name explaining my observations through terrorist propaganda. My gut feeling through my prayers as to what is going to happen in the future with Muslim extremist. The intuition within me that being of end-time prophecy and scenarios by this time it will be the Tenth anniversary of 911 and the terrorist will be making an effort too attack again this time I believe it will be by two fronts. They will attack by the Internet in an attempt to infiltrate computer systems in Pentagon and the Capital even missiles system sites. They will already have the smart bomb or the dirty bomb in place to be activated by computer on the Internet. The bomber could be overseas to activate the device or devices. Suicide bombers will be in place in the USA as back up in case of failure. They will walk in to said target and detonate themselves to set the dirty bomb off. Here's one reason why they will move from one to another. They will have to save face to young educated Muslims who have been told terrorists use smart people to blow themselves up. They will want to recruit the new generation of Muslims who have been learning about computers in the USA at Universities. Already they have many terrorist web sites that post coded messages to each other through their leaders speeches that get media attention throughout the world. If they would have pulled off a September 11th 2007 attack as they have threaten in that year. It will show they are in control it would have been small compared to what is coming up the pike. The democrats will have a seated president in 2008 wither a women or African American. A total insult to the Muslim extremist world would be a women president. After the 2008 elections into January 2009 we should know if we have fallen into more disfavors with the Muslims extremist. I hope this message will be taken heed to by then and we will have missed a major disaster. It will be in the hands of those that listen. We just might be able to prevent further extreme crashes to the economic well being of the Untied States and the world. Any added insults would stir up conspiracy theories everywhere. Americans will be told the Bush President is still in control and that this was done intentionally. That theirs no difference in democrat or republican they serve the same master. Some of that I believe but not for the same reasons I just believe we need a strong third party to rise-up and take away the controls. I'm not talking about Third

Reich type of party either something getting back to what this country was supposedly founded on.

The values of true believers in Christ the Bush administration has been compared to Hitler we don't even know what the genocide of a race of people is in the America most pure Europeans want to be blind to the fact what Europeans did to the Native Americans. So we would be desensitized to the holocaust because of our sheltered lives. We weep over the movies but easily forget when we go back to our real lives. We may start pulling out of Iraq in 2008 but the Extremist Muslims won't let us go they want to draw us into the confrontation. Looking for the back door like in computer hacking terms. They believe they are the chosen people to bring the great Satan down and there will be a One Muslim world order where all infidels will be wiped off the face of the earth. The New Kingdom on this Earth will be all Muslim oppressors they believe.

Such attempt will be futile because no religion on earth is 100% correct. Too many branches of beliefs breaking off everywhere I see December 21st 2012 as a rally point of the real world order where all mankind starts to see that we are all one. Muslim extremism will start to dwindle after the extreme attacks and failure of 9111. Because the warning will be out the right people will see. And maybe afterwards the real meaning of what Bono of U2 and Bill Gates proclaimed about eliminating the poor in the world will start to reign true. Because the rumors of war will dwindle and we can see peace for a change in a global arena.

War is what oppresses the people and takes love ones away. And causes misunderstandings of every type. The Muslims extremist would like to have their own Red Dawn where they drop out of the sky and take over America in the name of Allah and Mohammed. Our extreme climate change is because of war if you read the book "Beautiful Harvest." By this same author you will see that even back 2004 that even the government said that climate change was because of war we are living on a fragile system this big indigo Earth is alive with things to preserve us the all life. If we destroy everything by war the earth will just shake its foundations even more. Oil is the blood of the Earth like gold some would kill for it. By so doing if we let them they will kill us all like the fools they are dwindling our resources.

Gaming in Second Life:

Here in this chapter I'm dealing with factors of gaming in a virtual worlds secondlife as purely a example of what I'm talking about the collective mind of online gaming. Secondlife has many influences in the business world as I watched a program on discovery channel about all the revoluntionary possibilities. The follow is purely my opinion and speculation I'am not employed with secondlife and I'am not giving out cheating information on how to play. Here's the beginning of my speculation and research I say don't waste your time in Second Life with camping chairs and cleaning, saling yourself short as a drug dealer, prostitue, porno dancer, escort services. These are all dealing with things real life already has. The best way is to advertise objects that you've created like in real life there is no real short way to get money or L$ dollars as its presented in world. The best way is to use systums that you've learned about in real-life that are no where scrams or exhausted in the world. And use them in world or the virtual world your playing in at this time.

Set-up a store in world,learn about acceptable scripts in Second Life and use them with different shapes of things. I used a script for a car and a script for camping chair and put them together to create a camping chair cruiser. Now you don't have to sit in one spot you can cruise around in world with a Newbie or a friend and help them make L$.

Now, everything I've said about what not to do doesn't apply to what to do for yourself. If AV's want to buy camping chairs and gambling machines then you sale them to them. Sense this was written in my research I have found that gambling in secondlife.com has been shut down completely because internet gambling is illegal in the USA so they say I still see a lot of gambling sites online. This is something I never thought of relating to real-time advents. But over all I think it's a good thing sense I really don't believe you can control age limits online. A eight year old could say their 21 and no one would know until they told on themselves. Never-the-less some people do act like children online even when they are adults. There are still camping chairs where you can earn L$ cash. Saleing clothing that you'v made is easy. Just click on yourself and make clothing where ever it says create in world you'll learn how to do it.

Why use real life scams in second life? First of all the market in the real world is being exhausted and over rated at a alarming rate. While in a virtual world the economy is low and your dollars are bigger. Take the long running "No Money down." by Carlton Sheets.

His system has been around for years and eveyone who has bought it either for themselves or at your local yard sale. Everybody knows the information and are alerted to the content.

But guess what? In virtual world it works better because the exchange rate is so much lower and newer then just a few years. And accounts are flipping all the time so become a real-estate broker now is better. As of July 30th 2007 all Casino's where shutdown in Secondlife of which brought virtual world havic.

SL banks started shutting down because avatars where removeing L$ at alarming rates. I lost over L$2000 in game because of this which was only $10.00 in real-life. Banks in SL can open one day and be gone the next with your L$. I read somewhere online that SL employee stole about $20,000 for real. That's approximatly 2000 people per $10.00 so that amount adds up quickly. I wouldn't be surprised if it dealt with the Casino and SL Bank scare someone getting greedy.

Instead in SL Buy land if they are
flexible to sale, Rent, Buy, Sale, Trade.
Its an monopoly game that you can
franchise on because its an ever growing
market flip flopping and turning around.
Having a hard time moving it? Find out
who owns the most land in the area place
one of your most ugliest structure you
can on your land, a tall building with
no occupation useless. Accidently on
purpose place a spamming script on your
land that's set to launch at anybody who
gets near you even spamming on others
owners land. When your discovered and
you get many complaints you chalk it up
that you where learning script writing
it was a accident. You won't get a
warning about it from SL staff because
it's a first time offense. Now keep
building weird structures on your land.
You bought the land for L$6000 as a rule
sale it 3 times that much. Use the
number three for everything if they
won't take it for L$18,000 your bottom
line is L$9000 you want to sale for at
least L$3000 more then what you paid for
it. Now take that L$ and find more land
for L$6000 that takes at least 125
objects you don't want any covenants on
the land you want to be free to build
anything you want on it those rules in
this game are a joke trying similate the
real world. Buy this land and do the
same you did before. Don't stay in the
same area find other places that need a

fixer upper to come along. To buy many
cheap small peaces for L$2000 to put
them together for one whole peace of
land for 125 objects, lets say four
peaces of small land placed together
makes 125 objects you bought them all
for L$2000 now the cost of the land
combined is L$8000 add another L$3000
that's L$11000 to L$12000 is your
beginning asking price always round off
even then take bids or lower price as
you see fit. Don't sale less then L$9000
you must make your profit. In someplaces
you have to wait longer. Be patient it's
a waiting game sometimes. Start a
Contractor group where people sign-up to
be put to work like camping. Let them
sign-up for FREE but don't do a thing
with them. Only pay them 2% of your land
sales. You keep them employed and
playing the game. Payday could be few
and far in between but they'll have to
wait for your sales and big commission.
L$ stands for Linden dollars this is
what keeps the players playing.

Most people will wait some will press
hard to be put to work. Take one or two
of your crew set-up a camping chair at a
made up work site let them sit there for
a few hours. With cheap cost of some
land and so diverse AV personalities
can't wait to get out from some of it.
Don't spend time worrying about being
married on line figure out first how

make the L$ buy learning scripts and how use them, tweak the ones everyone uses, make better ideas from things already made. Additional things in the scripts by adding more scripts to one item you can have multitask funictionality. One script in one item is useless add more makes it a better item to sale.

Clothing is easy find your pics online upload them to your inventory and start making shirts, pants,shoes, by trying different pics you've loaded up. Something will fit into your own clothing line. Make-up fancy names and sale them on line same with tattoo's. Don't spend money on expesive books about second life either. There long and boring and tell you how to be a slut in second life.

Like in real life make yourself better in world then the outer world. In this edition I'll explore more about scripting with you. But for now just click around hit and miss like you can with a lot of software programs until you learn the system. It took me a week to figure things out and that was because I was fooling around with all the weopans and gadgets.

If your in a fantasy for to long you'll play role the fantasy in real-life. Your minds like a camera the image that appears in it will focus on your Soul. The character you become is the one that the shutter opens and closes on all the time. Until your actions appear in the real-world.

Remember in scripts its a numbers crunching game numbers in numbers out only one way to go in the law of averages in gambling online in the virtual world of scripts which for now is illegal online. Computer using is a learning process of how a computer funictions today. Using a binary system with adverb words the genius is to use the whole launguage. If you wish to have AI in the 21st century which will be achieved in part in a decade.

The Peek and Push Slotmachines in Sl and others like these no dought have lost a lot of business because of SL Casino shutdown. The worst of all and the most thought out locked scripts. You had to go after the slotmachines that really spin a lot and seem to have the same bell and handle sounds. There are so many different versions of this slot machine that when you pinpointed the script you knew the averages is in your favor. Something I noticed about this machine is that if you had one yourself in your own inventory you placed it on the ground and play it. If it seems to be really playing well for you then the same is true with others with in the SL Life.   But you must find the same machine or scripts in order for this to be true. At least in my theorie I maybe wrong. What does this tell you about Second Life? Everything is connected one way another even more so then in the material world. You find this out when you are looking for something it suddenly appears somewhere in world. You are playing within a scripted game with the same actions. It was written in a recent article I read before July 30th I believe the 1st that the FBI where welcomed to investigate SL for the casinos and gambling. It is for this reason because there is a real money exchange that they do so. SL must remember that they still have to abibe by the laws of the land. That's why they open there VR world to all to investigate. The Casino's have been damaged now frachises like the Peek and Push slotmachine business suffered no dought because they sold their scripted machines on E-Bay at auction. I heard some arrests might come down but where do you begin? With something that has been going on so long? I think it might be a threat but we'll see.

Rediscovering yourself

The purpose of this part of the book is to address issues of the self-discovery process and the author has used brief story subject lines to address the issue of addiction. Meanwhile the under line work is to help every person to find themselves back to who they are and there purpose in life in the real world. When Real time is expressed in support group sessions keep in mind the theme of Internet addiction runs hand in hand with natural and spiritual subjects. While others only experience a Spiritual addiction, perhaps cult experiences many will find subjects that can apply to other situations that may cause a person to be in oppression or obsessed with problems. David was in a cave with four hundred men who were distressed and in debt but later, they became mighty men and his warriors.

(1 Samuel 22:2) *"All those in distress, all those in debt, all those who had a grievance gathered round him and he became their leader. There were about four hundred men with him."* Now here we are in the 21st century facing the issues of modern times the cave being our home computer nest. This book puts a great deal of emphasis on the mentoring, sponsorship and role modeling. To raise up people in support groups to help our selves through knowing "who they are in

real time." With small groups helping to bring people into healthy relationships away from an Internet existence. Through the use of supports groups to talk out or to pray through the issues perhaps of self esteem, abuse, loneliness, addictions, rejection, and many other issues for today. Trying to build character through self- discovery and role model emulation through group leadership with a mind set not to rush through to many issues at one time. To coach groups helping them to move on with there own self-discovery.

In building, chapters or core groups the most important factor is to have people lead in the gifted areas of coach, guide counselor, and teacher.

In coming into a chapter our group is by, introduction by sponsorship. This person is in charge of helping to recover by discovering his/her next step in the growing process. For not keeping any person in the dark, as to what's next in the growing process. Of course, experience comes with the territory, this person has been down that road before drawing from experience, and they can help to coach along the way. This calls for mentoring and systematic work, making yourself available to your people. The man or women who takes this quest must be ready for the many challenges of being an open book to the people you deal with. The self-discovery and role model process of this book is based on the completion of and working with in their perception Journal including the personal passion statement. I have sighted several references off the Internet to support some of my research into the matrix of the Internet; this does not necessary mean they support my book they are sightings of support to my research only.

I am not responsible for any web links that may have been changed or re-routed online.

I plan to have a website where you can go to make update references to websites sighted here also to have recovery groups forums for those 24/7 surfers who are living introverted lives.

More about the Baby-boomer Generation

I write a lot about the Baby-boomer generation because I am a baby of the baby boomers the mere observer of the, Vietnam protesters, Wood-Stock, and a country looking for the wind of change to me they where confusing lazy times that made no difference to government war policy. They where persuaded by militant radical groups who had intentions to fuel terrorism of another kind feeding America in there drug culture as they continue today with all kinds of hybrid chemicals for the mind. Which I believe the changes have never happened because the one's who made the big fuss cut there hair and went into hiding as the yuppie generation or the like. We are paying for their message of Peace, Love, and Dove dope in our generation now. We created addicts and obsessions in the fiber of our generation.

Fixing the addictions of their generation of kids they have brought into their liberal mindset. That is for those who still are holding to what they took part of in those party days of our nation. I cannot stereo type all of them for some have raised themselves out of that mire and made good for what they stood for by contributing to society. We cannot say that all factions of a wannabe movement are the drug dealers of today but there are a few who still profit from their drug culture experiments. There are those who manufacture today's potent drugs abandoning even the thought of mind exploring or religious use feeding our generation from what they learned from the days past an undisciplined culture looking for profit fueled by foreign country's who hate North America for the freedoms it stands for. I look back to my days of party time during those times and see now more then ever who these people (drug dealers) where saying they where our friends.

I feel bad that I contributed to a selfish group seeking pure profit nothing to do with helping us go forward and I'm so glad now I have broken away from that with the help of my faith and other believers my addictions are few. Perhaps, I cannot say far and few in between because I believe that once you have experienced an addiction you must watch yourself for the next thing you can easily are drawn into.

Not necessarily, the same addictions there are many things that lurk in our human experience on earth. What does this have to do with computers you ask? Some of the yuppie generation have made good for themselves to inspire others to move forward into the future with

computer programming and computer
software and hardware to move our
country forward with healing, and
learning skills for the better of
humanity. To educate, to inspire the
next generation these are the building
blocks of a better learning curve,
Upwards and not on a downward spiral of
self-destruction.

Mental Health on the Web

There are many health problems that face the Internet user that have not even really been addressed to the fullest as of yet. Dealing with the back, wrest, and the eyes, including the mental health of people who are addicted to the net, you might have the occasional media fill in on the big boob tube looking to filling in coverage space. However, nothing to with overall lasting affects on curtain people with mental health problems. There is an effect not yet labeled the Internet has on a person I call it reality separation you can look this term up in my glossary of terms in the back of the book. This is a point of obsession where you believe a lie about yourself and your present circumstance. You are living in a reality relief of all sense of time and space. Like creating your own virtual reality of who you are in some cases there is total personality change mesmerized mind set to the things you involve yourself in on the net there are many self taught Internet hackers because of a duplication process in the learning curve. Your computer and the information highway can increase you IQ and the desire to learn it is tapping into the right resources, which should be and is the main concern of this book. Internet recovery is a process of deprogramming bad Intel from the good overcoming the dark with the light, working with offenders and those on there way in being first time offenders by what they learn.

We should take note here that many things can be conjecture this is a call for more research. The author has personalized this as he has experienced many of these symptoms first hand. He has seen marriages end up in divorces because of the double identity their spouse was living online.

Personally experiencing extreme swelling of the eyes and eye vision lost do to the over use of the computer and the Internet. Something most early computer manuals did not warn the user. Perhaps, fragments of information as these symptoms cropped up with new users.

Not to often do they address the problems those big corporations who manufactured the computers. They did not tell you in the beginning of the home computer systems the problems in some of the manuals of the computer when you brought it home and opened the package. Such as radiation from the computer screen to your eyes and the headaches from swollen eyes, some people would experience from over use of looking into a computer screen. Its a symptom of not blinking your eyes enough and you get

dry eyes ducks, needing to use eyewash
to help the fluid on your eyeballs. They
did not tell us in the beginning that
some the need for some of low radiation
screens such the CTL 5xn series by
energy star. Not everyone is affected
by this radiation blast from the
*computer screen that causes headaches in
the back of the head and around your
eyes, they have many other areas of
concerns to address. I believe the worst
effect is eye vision loss that is
speeded up by extreme use of the
computer; this symptom has been
connected with leukemia of which I
believe still needs further research
into rather then skimming over the issue
with simple media fill-in's.*

*Another concern should be the phenomena
of Flashes and Floaters or retinal eye
tear. There should be a study of people
who see flashes and floaters or spots in
front of their eyes do to prolonged
computer viewing. Media networks are
creating news by catching Internet
predators. The fact is many of these men
have been seduced by the Internet I'm
not trying to justify the problem.
Before you start wrecking these men's
lives first research into the cause of
the problem Yes, some of their very base
emotions have surfaced the causes of a
wicked heart. The power of the Internet
and mental suggestion is overwhelming.*

It is a haven of passing fantasy one after another the drawing effect of creating a new persona. You can be who you wont without anybody knowing the real you.

Liken to a compulsive gambler with his defenses down because he is on winning streak they may play until they're broke as they are lured into a false sense of security. Sense we are spending money catching these predators it is time to study the causes and effects of the Internet on mental health and behavior.

Moreover, help the many souls who are addicted to the Internet, who are shut-in's and display many symptoms of phobias from the outside world while they are living a introverted fantasy. It's only a matter of time with there weak mind deluded they want to carry it on in real-time. This same effect causes people who normally would not act out criminal acts to start role-playing on the Internet being addicted to stealing identity from unsuspecting friends, family, and strangers. Because they have a power to do so, feeling they are not denied anything at all. The Internet becomes a big game to play like god you can find out anything you want. You can control curtain aspects of people's lives they mess with you will mess with them. (Cyber Bullies) Some get into writing viruses, and Trojans, worms to impart their belief system that many times has been created by the dark side of Internet by other groups. You can be self-taught these things from off the Internet by hacker groups. Who set up websites for you to get your information, you can join their crusade never knowing their real identity. Often they play crude pranks on you. You think your downloading something for free while you're also downloading their Trojans or Worms on your system. On Coasttocoastam 09/17/07 George Noory read the news that some man had died of actual exhaustion in a Cyber Café of prolonged use of the computer. (See section on Computer stories and Urban Legends.) Again research must begin to realize the power of the introversion and the computer.

The Other identity Theft

This identity theft is the mind itself suffering from total detachment from the real world through a mod of fantasy that detaches itself from reality. Not much different then the late Howard Hughes whose world was fears and fantasy until the end of his time; The average computer operator cannot even start to imagine this thievery because there use is at an average perhaps four to five hours on the computer. While this other person is on the computer 24/7 not disconnecting from the net for one moment? They sleep by the computer leaving it only for awhile; some chat programs have alerts, beepers, pops, snap's, and crackles. To alert the user that someone is trying to contact them they wake up and in sleepy daze and go back to chatting on the Internet; this identity theft is lethal to mental health. We rush in with our new technology to teach our children at a very early age trying to better our children by the computer. The danger here is causing them to grow to fast, If we do not stop the practice of teaching the very young computers alone and not other curriculums of activity we will cause an age deficiency. (4) Take all your books about understanding People in there purest forms and start shifting the age level forwards kids at starting at 6 to 8 years primary ages try to shift to junior ages 9 to 11 by trusting in technology alone.

The effect seems great we will be teaching our children to be adults and genius before there time. For some will say hooray I will have my children out of the house sooner and they will be making more money then me. Moreover, they will take care of me the rest of my life when I'm old with all their great success. You cannot change human growth by introducing adult concepts early in child development. Look at what has happened to children who are aware of sex education at early stages of there life. An adult thinks if I introduce the birds and the bees by visual stimulation, I will have the subject out of the way. Some have introduced pornography to their children through adult books and reap the results by the many sex offenders who have been abused and have been abusers themselves. Abuse does not always mean a physical hand it can the mental challenge as well. Growing up in every century is becoming harder do to the challenges of technology it was hard enough for some in the nineteenth century to handle the new math.

Its natural precession is a computer and new communities of people worldwide communicating around the world with all kind of thoughts and theories everywhere. Finding out what is on the dark side of humanity as the dark side of the moon, the details are fuzzy until the light shines on the issue.

So you are saying computers are bad? Technology is bad? No. Let us put it this way if you remember the gun right's slogan "Guns don't kill people, People do." Then you'll have some of the concept of what I' m saying about computers in today's society. The old school taught many of us well by teaching us to work hard. Falling short of really trying to build natural ability perhaps, all you have heard was work for the man sale your self to him.

He will take care of you if you work hard? It did not solve the problem when many veteran workers where laid off loosing there pensions short one or two years until retirement. Interestingly enough those very same people have to be retrained to suite the New World coming. As I've said before I' am a researcher, observer, and a predictor by my research I see a bad trend coming as the Baby Boomer generation becomes our new senior citizens a new effect is on there children.

It involves a new detachment from the world of reality into a world of fantasy of which for us in North America we are the masters of new thinking. We are twenty years from the virtual thinking the computer will bring us into a new reality. Even today, we are already trying to incorporate computers into our cars and we have not even begun to figure out the full effects of cell phones on the millions of people that use them. Now we are plugging the computer into our car and having it interactively communicate with us the car and a satellite. We have not started to address this community of zombies and introverts on the Internet. The cell phone radiation on the brain has been addressed more then that of our pride and joy of the computer. Oh we hear step away from the computer, rest your eyes, stretch, and have a breather. The amazing thing the people who have nine to five jobs working fast pace schedules cannot have the luxury of such a break without loosing there jobs. Then even more amazing they take their computer home with them to do more work. The Future Shock is truly upon us in these days and times if we do not slow down we will literally burnout before our time. For some will say that truly this is our time, the time of man in his glory is at hand. We can make ourselves livelong, be younger, and perhaps defeat early death by our technology? Do we think faster is better? How fast do we go?

The New Matrix

Sometime in the near future of the 21st century in next five to ten years a new Internet operating system will be running as the result of Internet hacking, phishing, virus's, code breaking. In the effort toward off the ever-growing threat of cyber terrorism this will be the excuse to create an elite group into the Matrix. What we perceive as our present reality that computers will now fuel simple simplistic reality of nano chip technology. The Internet has created a new deception the autonomous anonymous which creates a persona of who you want to be either male or female good or bad. Not much different then the science fiction Movie Matrix, when it is Neil who lives a double life one in cyber space and the one in present body of the material world. The very same persona that has duplicated itself on the Internet this persona figure is becoming an ever-growing problem for the FBI and other like intelligent groups worldwide. With the creation of worms, Trojans, viruses, tweaks and preaks, cracks, phishing swindlers who gain unlawful or fraudulent access to financial information of individual's financial information through fake web sites. We quickly are creating another addiction for the entire world to embrace. Not just to pornography, as many mainstream Christian and Muslim media perhaps would like to point out but new characters in a reality, as the non-technology world knows it to be.

It is like the experience of new higher being in our safety zone picking and choosing characters in our play.

We have achieved the greatest tool humankind has ever experienced the Internet, the information highway, the world archive. Going at a marvel rate into faster means of communication it has its bloggers, forums, chat room sometimes information gets out to the world before the media has even finished the day pumping out there News here comes new media.

Look at the propaganda, conspiracy theories fueled by misinformation it can be a hit and miss search of information never the less we have created the biggest archive in our information highway that you can ever imagine.

"Wait I stand corrected." An information Highway that is still being paved beyond our imagination because it is fueled by imagination and it is not even finished yet. In my perception, we are in the wake of the third generation matrix. The first came before 1995 with the industry of the IBM, Commodores, Apple, Sinclair and the weeding out of the new technology to those things, which would stand the market the baby boom of computers. Things that shaped our first interest in computers; I have used every one of these systems or have owned them in that era. The second wave starting booming after 1995 after I purchased my first major 486 Operating system; because I discovered my Computer was on sale at Wal-mart I soon found out my great error was that it was already obsolete. From that point was my discovery of the Internet. I have been on it ever sense and have studied the trends of this great communication device it is ironic that the beginnings of my home computer started with Wal-Mart that embraces the new microchip technology of today. Within this time, I was babe in the second matrix but with the help of fellow surfers and my computer helping me along the way I soon expanded my knowledge and started teaching my self-HTML programming, Java Script and the like now I have web pages. I'm a webmaster. Personally, I wanted to get into gaming programming creating computer software. But was inpatient in the long programming and mathematics of it all leaving that to the genius's out there that have the time and an early start on the careers to do so believe me this field you should start when you are in the prime of your youth. I could probably build a new gaming program within a month I boost that I can figure out any program without a manual within an hour at least the basics and have it fully functioning with in a week. You soon start developing within your computer who you are if after years of using it you go back to see everything you have saved you will find the character you have created. Look for the junk things that should be deleted but before you do ask yourself why did I keep it anyway?

For what reason did this influence me? Was it a peace of spam mail?

Perhaps a friend who gave me some software? This is why law enforcement ceases computers when they are investigating you for your Internet activity, it tells a whole a lot about your mind set in short the computer is becoming more like you with the information you put on the hard drive. The third wave of the Matrix is soon to be divided towards the lesser and the greater operating systems and how much money you want to invest into your computer habits. It will be leaning towards safe guards in the system from prying eyes and those who have nothing else to do then form elite Internet groups to disrupt the way we do business in real-time. The week of June 6 2006 many where made aware of what they call Net-Neutrality from the media. This is

the pivotal point of the new order of
things to come on the net. We may win
the first battle. Nevertheless, are we
ready for the next wave? Dealing with
this issue of our right to surf where we
want too. Freedom of speech advocates
will have their day of protest. Because
of corporate seduction of the net, these
conglomerates are trying to figure out
ways to make more money off the Internet
and the consumer user. The new
generations of users are not aware of
tangled web loosed on them as they surf.
They are the new fuel that feeds the
melding pot. The new system is not
Microsoft's alleged LongHorn program
either it is under raps or being tested
somewhere in the USA and the United
Kingdom. I have no paperwork or Intel to
this system yet, other then symbolic
gestures of the times both biblical and
scientific protocols. I have had dreams
of the system in operation that cased
global sanctions as never seen before.
Humankind has written in his fictional
accounts about the end times and
machines taking over the world and being
his dictators. The first battlefront we
must win before innocent people are
pulled inward to the new system and
loose their ability to be who they
really are is the battle for the mind.
Recovery does not mean to stop using the
computer or the Internet it means
raising up computer savvy users with all

the right information. Intervention from the dark side of the Internet we will always need someone to be knowledgeable on how to break free from the snares of the dark widows' web. We have the independent hacker groups that form on the web who figure there in the game for good. Clubs and web gangs of organized web griefers who choose antonymous anonymous as a front to which to operate: For some it is a game for others they think there making a difference for whatever movement they represent.

I conclude this section of the book and leave you with some other information I got off the web. Please be advised keeping a real-time journal is important for a computer user. Record your thoughts because you will loose some information inside your computer and may never return to them until a later point in time. It is important to record your feelings at the various intervals of time in your Internet experiences on your computer. You will be surprised by your education level and thought processes within a year's time. Be honest with yourself am I growing in this experience or have I sunk into some undesirable thinking that will cause pain to others and myself around me. While we desire to escape the real world, we enter another the same way we left the first, with the same old wrecking ball we had. My study of virtual worlds is that there is always a backdoor to leave but you cannot run from yourself.

If the Internet has not, be a positive thing in your life then you should leave it alone because it is a destructive force to your mental health.

I call this a god-like syndrome you created this persona on the Internet and you feel powerful by being this person. While in real life your, someone else perhaps feeling the lowest on the totem pole with no way out. However, online you are this master of your domain type of person; and for some they have carried it back into the real world believing they are this in control person they created online.

Then the whole world comes crashing down on them and they find out how weak minded they really have been. When a reporter walks in the room and asks them what they are doing here. Suddenly, reality comes back to them to the person they are or who they have become and it is not so easy to escape.

A study of a person's mental health when the eyes are cued to a chat room or a virtual world and the ego being stroked and shaped into another being created by depravity. From day one, take a person who seems to live a normal life and see what they are like from a year from now, exposed to the whims of the net.

That is the importance of a personal journal study yourself be honest with yourself ask yourself am I happy with the person I am online would I survive in the real world? If you question any of these things and your self-serving.

I suggest you put the Internet away and adjust to the real world. Maybe find counseling if you take yourself too seriously in online chat rooms and virtual worlds. Many of people have judged themselves by a faceless relationship online that they are unworthy. These people if they have felt anything to do with suicide feelings or revenge, wanting to do acts of cyber terrorism. Should step away from the computer and the Internet and seek counseling. It is just too easy for you to be caught up in many moments of meaningless pleasure dampened by default. If I may suggest here the computer will expose your inner feelings latent to the power of the soul. If you are a deceptive personality it will bring it to the surface sevenfold if you have any addictive personalities this will surface in a matter of time. This can be for the good of adjustments or it can serve to mal-adjustments of personality. That is why I suggest computer users step away from the computer if they are fixed on it as there only social outlet.

Learn to be more extroverted and out going in positive refreshing ways rather then inverted in a world of dazzle.

Concluding remarks.

Is there as real end time scenario here? In this book I have explored the gamete of everything I know of at this present time about the Internet and the future of information highway and about mental health issues.

In this I may have alluded to my Spiritual Faith. We know about the end-time scenarios of anti Christ and mark of the beast. We've heard that of the super computer in Europe called the beast. We have read many books about the crashing economy like "The Day the Dollar Dies." Willard Cantelon in the Christian world.
Alarmist like "When Your Money Fails: y Fails: The "666 System" is here by Mary Stewart Relfe with the same everywhere the outcome of nothing is the same even though it appears things are happening we can't live paranoid lives. The Religious extremist from even the Christian world can see little details of something and read something massive into nothing. Like the Y2K scare that many men of God put their ministry on

the line for to make money on a few end-
time books. While not all where on the
bandwagon and where seemly ignorant to
computer facts I'm sure a new generation
is now more alerted. We haven't had
groups of people take their computers
and burn them in pile yet or bash them
with slug hammers that I know of as of
to date. On that supposed day of Y2K I
hosted a New Years vigil to light a
candle after midnight. To show we are
the lights of the world and no computer
crash will stop the good news of Christ.
I posted on my web site at that time
that my prediction was right. You
wouldn't have heard of me I was a lowly
preacher in Montana didn't have any
major book out. So am I saying computers
are bad? Christians shouldn't be
involved with them? If you have read
that into this book I'm in hopes to
clarify in these last remarks. The key
is in the verse by the bible which is
futuristic I believe that tells all
about where you are to be. No matter how
far advance man becomes in his
discoveries. Some true believers are
going to be there to prove the existence
of God. To proclaim I'm that I'm. It's
these words in the New Testament that
tells it all. "Put on the full armor of
God." IT starts out with the helmet.
Why? First of all this is where the
battlefield begins. In VR it will be a
helmet type device that covers the head.

Where all intelligence and creativeness
begins. We create our own world there
are no consequences God is our creator.
The battle will be for the Godsend
consciousness to rein. Where intelligent
beings try to take over with global
consciousness to do wrong. The God-
senders will counter act the virus or
worm of information that would try to
devastate us. If we where to be
challenged to take the mark of the beast
our computer soldiers would crack the
code. We are entering an era that every
word matters. Transcending time and
space because the evolution of mankind
is so much greater then before. The true
awaking of the consciousness of man by
the power of the Holy Spirit. Those
gifts we are given will be far greater
then before. I can't even start to
remind you dear Christian stop having a
defeatist attitude. There is a
stronghold in Christianity that says we
must die literally like Christ in the
physical to be worthy of him. That we
will be defeated on earth and rise again
like him. I tell you a new era is being
ushered in that we don't have to be
defeated we can raise our head up high
and be counted worthy to be like him the
son's and daughters of God. Through the
metamorphosis of life changing surrender
being defeated has ended. I'm not
interested in the study of vanishing
races like the Incas because I'm not

surprised that such practice of sacrifice would meet its demise.

Why wouldn't the creator be a jealous God when we sacrifice what he has created and tempt God all over again? A sheltered community trying to hide from the whims of society will no longer be able to hide from the intruders of life, the predators and identify thieves. Already we see Christian community's being invaded by predators in the news hiding ourselves in a closet will not make it all go away. Four walls and the comfort zones won't cut it in the future. Yes, there is always a price to pay for what you believe. This is the greatest visual generation to come to our world to live by example will reign true even more. The forefront for the battle of the minds is at hand not to be a mindless spineless generation full of zombies. Bible decoders got some of the puzzle right when they say this is the age when the secrets of the bible will be revealed. A time such as this that those things hidden will help aid humankind in his quest on this big indigo planet. The bible code at this time has its flaws in logical dissemination. Human error still equates it usefulness to stop disasters before they happen. But in time the right researcher will figure it out the one who's in the God-senders Squad. In everything that humanity has created there has always been the darkness and the light. This remains so for this great technology age that is rushing before us. We have our soldiers of light that will aid in great rescues of people lost to the dark side of the Internet. Almost sounding like the matrix the movie because in this race are those who still believe and who are ready to take back what darkness has taken to bizarre levels.

Stories of the Computer.

In this section I dedicate it to Internet nightmare stories on the Internet perhaps urban legends. This section of the book will be updated as I work on a new edition for future reading. This is only an example of some stories about computers.

Man dies using laptop at wheel

27/02/2007 07:27 - (SA)

Yuba City, California - A man who authorities say appeared to be driving while using his laptop computer died on Monday when his vehicle crossed into oncoming traffic and collided with a Hummer.

After the crash, California Highway Patrol officers found the victim's computer still running and plugged into the cigarette lighter of his 1991 Honda Accord.

The 28-year-old victim was a computer tutor. The Sutter County coroner's office was withholding his identity until his family could be notified.

"The screen itself shattered from the impact, so we can't be sure if he was working on it or not, but we think from the way it was found that he might have been working," CHP spokesperson sergeant John Pettigrew said.

"It's a straight road right there, and it doesn't look like he fell asleep or anything else."

This is not all that uncommon I've seen people with cell phone in one ear laptop on the seat or dash board of the car and their weaving all over the highway like someone who's been drinking. I saw one person who had her map spread out looking at it while talking on the cell phone. She was all over the highway weaving to the shoulder to the center line needless to say if had been a patrolman I would have pulled her over and gave her a citation with no regret.

Korean man dies after computer games binge (The Age)

October 10 2002

A 24-year-old South Korean man died after playing computer games non-stop for 86 hours, police said yesterday.

The jobless man, identified by police only by his last name Kim, was found dead yesterday at an Internet cafe in

Kwangju, 260 kilometers southwest of Seoul, they said.

Quoting witnesses, police detective Oh Myong-sik in Kwangju said the man had been virtually glued to the computer since late last Friday and had no decent sleep and meals.

The man collapsed in front of the counter early yesterday but soon regained consciousness. He then went to the toilet where he later was found dead, the police officer said.

Initial investigation ruled out the possibility of murder, police said. An autopsy was planned. South Korea is among the world's most Internet-savvy nations with more than half of its 47 million people having access to the Internet. South Korea has some 22,000 Internet cafes, also known as PC rooms.

Many PC rooms are open 24 hours, but no minors are allowed after 10 p.m. Remember when Jobe was sucked into the mainframe VR computer in the Lawnmower man? This reminds me of the exhaustion it would take for such a thing to happen. The human body could never handle it let alone the endurance of radiation. Like Star Treks teleporter you would have to figure out how change the molecule structure of the human body to transport like the Movie Tron into the computer. If such technology would exist it would be way into the 22nd Century until such a thing could be acquired. Some have said that stories of old like this one are Urban legends this second story confirms the samething. Is it yet another Urban legend? I don't think so I know first there are health issues I haven't even addressed yet.Chinese man dies after week-long gaming session by James posted on February 28, 2007 12:26pm

After spending "almost all" of the week-long Lunar New Year holiday playing videogames, a 26-year-old, obese man in Northeast China collapsed and died on Saturday. State-run media calls the

The "China Daily" report quotes a local teacher who blames the man's death on the "dull life" the holiday creates. The teacher says people have just two choices for entertainment when all markets and café are closed: TV or Error! Hyperlink reference not valid.. State media reports about 2.6 million, or 13%, of China's 20 million Internet users under 18 are considered addicts. (From geek.com)

Some stories say 50 hours instead 60-80 hours the question is when does the endurance of being online effect your mental health?

I still wander if this is a rekindle of the former story like an urban legion. I question of performance enhancing drugs where involved. A story that should be told and have yet to find it is that using the computer increases intelligence.

I believe that this is my own story, which will not go into detail about here. But sense I've used the computer it has helped my writing skills and my mathematics. Perhaps this study I will place here a future editions of this book.

Global approach needed on cybercrime: experts by Staff Writers
Geneva (AFP) Oct 5, 2007
Telecoms and computer executives, legal officials and UN agencies on Friday warned that the world needs to take a global approach to tackling cybercrime and security issues on the Internet.

International Telecommunications Union chief Hamadoun Toure said individual national or regional approaches to tackle spam, hackers, remote attacks on computer systems and use of the Internet for crime would inevitably be flawed.

"Cyber security is a global problem and it needs a global solution," he told journalists after a meeting here.

The attempt to set up a global agenda to tackle cybersecurity has gained momentum following a concerted wave of cyber attacks on Estonia's websites and computer infrastructure in May, participants said.
"It can happen again, anywhere in the world," said Norwegian judge and computer crime specialist Stein Schjolberg.

"Whatever applies in the conventional world can apply in an amplified way in the cyberworld," he added.

The meeting decided to set up five working groups to examine possible legislative and technical measures, more international cooperation and reinforcing finance and security infrastructure.

Toure said the experts were aiming to report on their findings next March, and he would introduce recommendations on concrete steps at an ITU council meeting in September 2008.

Even before I conclude the writing of
this book already steps are being made
towards a New Matrix. A New World order?
We are creating our own reality on the
information highway what happens there
is being carried out in reality. In
solving our problems we always hope we
don't create another one.
There's always someone who wants
control. Let me briefly mention here
another term for the Matrix is used in
what is called TRV or Technical Remote
viewing something I personally have
experienced on the Internet. Yes, long
term use of the computer I believe can
stir up this latent power of the soul.
Without being present with someone
hundreds of miles away you pick pictures
of things about them information about
their present state of being. Briefly,
as I don't want you to think this to be
a lecture on how to do it. All I can say
here is that after prolonged use of
Internet. You will find out some new
skills you have picked up. It's like
body language through typing, and
viewing through seeing into the computer
screen. I have experienced this
phenomenon many times over in locating
people, and praying for pacific needs.
While this is not being physic it is
spiritual and natural. You experience
the true meaning of Super-Natural.
I feel this is better then the use of a
pin and paper to draw images. The

combination of both skills obviously
would work the best. I offer no right or
wrong here in the observation I only
brought it out to you as further
research into the computer world and
stories of the computer.
I do believe mans Spirituality is
growing in new leaps and bounds. Only I
don't believe it's through old school
religion or the occult I see a pure
awaking of the mind without props,
ritual and form.
When we can learn to practice the
presence of God, and still our minds.
We will see greater works happening for
the growth of the humanity.
Again I offer no great scholarship here
only opinions set for other book
material I might write later.
In practice I'm in hopes of making aware
the usefulness of the Internet and how
we can make the ignorant aware that its
not just a game but a tool to advance
humanity towards a better future. And
how we can be apart of the solution and
not the problem.
Education is the key to discipline not
shock treatment but cooperation.
Old school discipline is like the
military yelling at the top of your
voice to fear a sense of god into your
being. This simply doesn't work in child
growth they either learn to be abusers
and hate you continuing to act as past
generations creating a dysfunctional

family. Hate and resentment can cause a
breach of the soul damage beyond repair.
Self-image is the key to growing a
better environment. A person acts the
way they do because their environment so
often is a mirror reflection when
someone ventures into the Internet
world. They find the fuel to continue
their dysfunctional environment. The key
is intervention to the bad habits that
are so easy to pick up on the Internet,
cyber world or an environmental window.
Sense writing this chapter I relay
another story of the Internet. On our
local news here Montana it was said that
there was estimate of 32,000 sex
offenders on MySpace alone. Parents are
being alerted to monitoring their
children online activities as they lured
by these predators. Again I cannot
stress the importance of education for
this fast pace tool such as the computer
and the Internet it's no longer a game
it involves impressionable minds. That
at early age nothing shocks them that
much anymore when it deals with the
Internet. Look at Myspace and Youtube
what they post on the net you'll be
shocked the open information that is
advertised on those places.

"How to write a Lifeline Journal."

Feel free to express yourself in your journal about how you feel about things being a computer and Internet user. Don't worry about every situation and don't get hung up on it like it's a crutch. In a group situation, you can share from your journal with other people in the group. Do so as to add to the conversation, discuss your feelings about being a computer user good and bad experiences. Think about stories to share ever so briefly and not naming to many names or to many details. All for the purpose of self-discovery of whom you are as a person compared to the one you express on the Internet. The self-discovery comes through the adventure, things that can be found out about yourself right were you are at. Remember society in general sees discipline through a different set of eyes. Your job here is to hear from the others in the group and their experiences and overcoming problems. Iron sharpens Iron so the bible says sharpen each other through the relationships you encounter, help each another by being the true friend.

Share only what you desire to share out of your journal this is usually a private affair working through your Personal thoughts. See the Appendix

for further study of journal writing
And its purpose. (Journal Genie)

Glossary of Terms

This maybe layman's terms of use but will help nevertheless to get up a basic program understanding. To see script on paper like a schematic electronic board can help to fit the peaces of the puzzle together. Sometimes you must learn to borrow some logic to improve on another. Looks at other scripts how they have been written take the same program and learn from it by changing things within it. Soon you will see how each of these words fit into the logic of the script.

While this list isn't complete with all SL scripting language the point being that some words in the 80's have carried onto this present generation of programming. It shouldn't be hard for advanced users to pick script writing up within the program.

I do not profess to know it all about script writing and I' am still learning. But the basics are where we all have to begin, if you have some additional comments that will help contribute to this book please feel free to send your constructive thoughts my way to improve on this book. Such as to better define the terms here feel free to e-mail me with your improvements. I believe that within this study you will find that the conclusion of the matter about programming to match binary code that it all deals with the principle of cause and effect One effects the other by the users choice. Somewhere in the great secret of things this knowledge will be used to defeat the great Colossus computer that Christians have called the beast throughout end-time history. This part of the book is in simplest of terms a Computer Technician would see humor in this because it lacks the arithmetic's of the functionality of code source. This is the simplest way just understood terms you might pick up a small portion of script writing in a Virtual World. I recommend you find classes that deal with the computer science if you want to pursue further study. Sharpen your math abilities before taking advance courses, you can go to private classes as well. This is fast pace changing field you need to get started as soon as you can and it will be a constant upgrade of knowledge to keep up with the new technology.

Computer Lexicon

Not in alphabetical order

VR: Virtual Worlds like worlds.com and secondlife.com With a UI interface. While the real Virtual reality hasn't been completely achieved yet in this fast pace world the virtual headset for such worlds is being thought out without a doubt within SL with voice recognition. Its just been integrated as I wrote this part of the book.

AI: Artificial Intelligence where the computer takes on human like qualities and is able carry out commands by its own design with human like logic without User command Actions. The future UI for Virtual Worlds will be used for Security issues and running scripted objects within world at first. Being a branch of computer science concerned with building computer C.P.U. That imitates human thought processes threw Free will and decision making through commands Programmed by users. (*Cause & Effect*) The renegade robot hasn't been invented yet but truly a man without God the creator is lost and destine to destroy himself with his own technology tinker toys.

UI: User Interface is the Users view of in world activity. It is used for communication with in other VR Worlds to build objects and to surf to other land within world In this case to other scripted chat worlds are common links between system components allowing many more systems to link together via ISP. In other words this is what you see your world threw like a browser IE or Netscape, or Mozilla Firefox but without therewith an integrated program within the program.

If: word which asks a question and waits for a user response to resolve the condition to post further action within components in a system. Usually a True/False response

Index: displays a list of files or programs that could be on your CPU or a management system such as for building web sites.

Indexed file: is a file stored on a retrieval system such as a computer.

Information: Data that answers the user's question such as the term information highway.

Information highway: Information a computer user searches on the Internet. Presently in theory 75% chances are you will find users who believe like you. Nothing is really that unique everything in life will tell you something.

Initialize: to start a scripted program from the beginning. Or to re-boot it to test intermediate changes that they are correct

Input: anything that contributes to the overall function of the computer system by floppies, keyboard or other devices.

Integer: is variable in FORTRAN, a series of not more than six characters.

ARRAY: A group of logically sequential memory spaces in which data can be stored. (ICS1980)

EDIT: Every creating software program should have the edit command. It helps to add, and makes changes or even delete the document to start all over again. Or file that is obsolete or needs modifications. In SL case some commands have been deleted for good they proved to be of no use or causing problems with grid functionality. Their web site tells a lot about these banned commands.

LET: The statement that assigns a value to a variable.

STRING: Characters that function together as an overall unit.

FLOAT: A condition of computer calculation in which the CPU keeps track of the decimal point within the script as the arithmetic-logic unit.

SAVE: the instructions to save data on the hard drive, floppy, or any copy device compatible with the system operations. Has been a consistent command of computers from early conception of the world of home and office computing.

SET: a verb used manipulating indexes such a status physics true or false in SL.

MoveTo: to shift said data from one vector to another vector target.

POS: one or more vectors used to pass information in a scripted program. Often used with a Target vector within the script.

Matrix: A system to determine the spatial location of points by reference to horizontal and vertical coordinates. (Ics Supplement 1980)

NEXT: The Statement concluding a FOR/NEXT loop. (ICS1980)

COPY: To instruct to duplicate programs, or to file it onto a floppy disk, or CDR disk.
DEFAULT: In scripts this is pre-established setting for various variables in the script.
DELETE: uses to erase useless files or programs on a CPU or a scripted program on notepad or any word processor used to establish script.

DIAGNOSTICS: Either a program to check computer hardware and search for malfunctioning parts. Human tracing components but can also is often done apply (ICS19080) or this to diagnostics of functioning script. The user runs the script through software program to see if functions like he created it to.

DOWNLOAD: To copy files from host computer, usually a mainframe, to a personal computer. This concept is used when computers are linked together in some network. (ICS1980) In 21st century terms the Internet.

DOWNTIME: The period of time it takes for SL upgrades its software usually resulting in a new download with updates. Also the grid is shut down for maintenance, and repairs, etc. I believe I have found that VR worlds have to have this when the population grows at overwhelming rate. Look at a 512 floppy disk now think about it you are buying this land or island for space on someone's mainframe. In real life its no bigger then that floppy. Some pay over $1450 for several spaces. SL is limited to Windows XP for Windows operators of whom I believe to be a mistake and will prove to be fatal when Microsoft upgrades to a more sufficient System other then Vista. Perhaps the Longhorn System unless Bill Gates is partners in world and is working on that with SL.

You just don't know what's working behind the scenes in big business.

RETURN: instructs program to go back to a subroutine.

SUBROUTINE: a subsidiary route within a script used as needed during the execution of the program.

This could be by True/False statements used by the user.

SCAN: To search any array, as to determine the frequency of certain character traits of script. This can be added onto other statements to make it True/False function within a subroutine or the like.

STATUS: used in processing the data within the script after a servicing of an interrupt. Again dealing with True/False statements within the script.

INTERRUPT: A deliberate break in the script normal flow or routine usually accomplished by script True/False statements. Or and involuntary interrupt such as a total crash of the computer do to electric power outs. Sometimes resulting in complete loss of data not saved.

WHILE: Condition this executes as true then loop.

Loop can be either a single statement block statement, or null statements.

ELSE: The element of an IF/THEN statement that causes alternate processing when condition is FALSE.

(ICS1980)

NULL: (From Wikipedia.org)
Null is a special pointer value (or
other kind of object reference) used to
signify that a pointer intentionally
does not point to (or refer to) an
object. Such a pointer is called a null
pointer. Many implementations use a
value of 0 (all bits zero) to represent
the null pointer, as this is at the
bottom of the address space of most
CPUs.

Variable: Symbol used to represent a value
or group of values within a computer
program that can change as the program
is executing. (ICS1980)My own personal
note here: Throughout the years of
advancement those values can be modified
before the program is executed scripting
in virtual world is a good example of
this process. In some cases it can make
the program run faster or perhaps run
like a virus, Trojan, or a worm
depending on the creators intentions for
it to run.

Hackers Glossary

1.   Exploit—A noun that refers to a program that demonstrates or takes advantage of a software security hole. Writing an exploit is the best way to technically describe a security hole while simultaneously demonstrating it. That is why "White Hat" hackers (hackers who use their skills to help companies discover security problems) often write exploits.

2.   Root—As a noun, refers to cyber omnipotence, the highest-level o access on a computer. Can also be used as a verb. "To root a box," means to obtain root through unconventional means, at which point the system has been "rooted."

3.   Haxored—A cool underground term for hacking. "I haxored the box."

4. Trojan—Shorthand for "Trojan horse," a method of cracking a system by slipping it a seemingly harmless and beneficial program that secretly contains programming that gives an attacker unauthorized access. Common off-the-shelf Trojans include Back Orifice 2000, and Sub-7, recently spotted masquerading as a free Internet adult film—beware of Greeks bearing porn.

5.   Eleet—means "elite," but generally used with sarcastic or self-deprecating

humor and spelled out with numerals, not roman letters: 31337. "I hax0red this box with 31337 skillz," might mean, "This was too easy."

6.   Rootkit—A generic term for a suite of programs that gives a hacker fun things to do after rooting a box. Might include programs for covering your tracks or for "sniffing" a company's network for interesting traffic.

7.   Zero days—a security hole that has been discovered underground, but not yet by the computer security community.

8.   Docs—A person's identifying information, like name, email address, social security number, etc. "I rooted his box and downloaded his docs."

9. Script kiddie—someone who uses exploits to penetrate unsecured Boxes, deface websites, and generally make trouble, without having the skills to write such a program themselves usually a juvenile.

10. Packet monkey—a script kiddie who floods computers and websites with data packets, to maliciously take them offline. The distributed denial of service attacks that sometimes afflict popular (See Appendix Security Focus)

The Authors additions

**11. Net-Neutrality: What's this all about? Big phone and cable companies are trying to get rid of Network Neutrality, the fundamental principle that prevents them from discriminating against your favorite Web sites and services.

Our broad coalition wants to keep the Internet free and open for everyone. Go to http://www.savetheinternet.com
** This is only a surface problem things like this already exist for communist countries, and countries other then the USA and Great Britain. I have been told by a person in Ghana Africa that there are some stringent controls which for now I will leave this alone for I don't want to reveal my future source for another book I'm writing.
**12. Cyber Bullies: also they can be put in the class called griefers. They have their own brand of terrorism. If you ever have one of these on your trail they can make your life miserable. They will put you on e-mailing lists; they will spam your cell phone. If your business has a website they will send fictitious mail to it in your name to get you in trouble. They will send advertisements to you and sign you up on every annoying web business you can find. They will post slander about you your picture even doctored pictures like

porno. Put your name on the false pic that they created to represent you on the Internet. Heaven for bid if they ever get your bills, your phone number your friend's phone numbers, and your identity of any kind. They have many excuses if they get caught. The best defense is that they have an e-mail worm. And they just erased your information off their computer. They will make up stories about you in chat rooms that you frequent, erase your account information and change all your e-mail address's to eliminate them. If they live in the same city or town alert the court system perhaps get a retraining order if they are a physical threat. Use sound and video cams to catch the culprit to use as evidences against them. Everything must be documented in order to get any charges against these freaks. It takes lots of money for any agency to trace them. That's why so many hacks get away with things on the Internet it cost too much to pursue them. This is gradually narrowing down, as law enforcement agency's become more aware of the crimes and how to catch the criminal mind on the Internet.

Worm: A is a computer program that can copy itself and infect a computer without permission or knowledge of the user. The original node may modify the copies or the copies may modify themselves, as occurs in a metamorphic node. A virus can only spread from one computer to another when its host is taken to the uninfected computer, for instance by a user sending it over a network or the Internet, or by carrying it on a removable medium such as floppy disk, CD, or USB drive. Additionally, viruses can spread to other computers by infecting files on a network file system or a file system that is accessed by another computer. Viruses are sometimes confused with computer worms and Trojan horses. A worm can spread itself to other computers without needing to be transferred as part of a host, and a Trojan horse is a file that appears harmless until executed. Here is a list of terms I put as simple as possible. May I suggest that you go to the Internet search engines like Yahoo, Google, Wikipedia and look up these terms for further study?

(From http://en.wikipedia.org)

** FireWall: Software designed to block unwanted entry into the ports of your computer. Set for network priorities to prevent network intrusion.

**Cracks: This is usually information you find on the Internet to cheat at a game on a CD's perhaps some virtual games. It might tell you to type in a code in window of the program to give infinite power to overcome your enemies. There are many examples of this term it would be too exhaustive to enter in this volume of this book. Another use is to remove protection methods of shareware, trial, or demo software essentially you get the full function of the software without buying the license. It removes the annoying pop-up screens to purchase or its about to expire. Many companies now have placed trick counter measures to cracks. If you enter the numbers it might disable the software completely making it hard for you to figure the program out.

**Serials: These are the codes you get for unlocking shareware, or trial software programs. You by pass purchasing the product and enable all its features for free. The problem about getting on these web-sites is that you might be sent cookies with intentions of leaving spyware on your computer.

**Keygens: These programs you download from Warez sites that enable you to find key numbers and letters to unlock software that is meant to be purchased. But you get them free by the key-gen program configuration. Again the problem is you are taking the chance of downloading viruses, worms, Trojans, and spyware. Thus you pay the price for something you get for free and is illegal.

**Spyware: Usually a cookie that is scripted to keep track on you or software that has been installed without the users knowledge. In some cases it collects your information right off your computer if you do not have a Firewall in some cases it can take over your computer by locking it up to load their software on your computer. It monitors the user behavior. These programs will send out pornography pop-ups to your computer screen that's why you have a firewall and virus scanner program with spyware search abilities.

"Warez" refers primarily to works traded in of copyright law. The term generally refers to illegal releases by organized groups, as opposed to peer to pee file sharing between friends or large groups of people with similar interest using a darknet.

It usually does not refer to commercial for-profit software counterfeiting. This term was initially coined by members of the various computer underground circles, but has since become commonplace among Internet users and the mass media(From Wikipedia.org)

**Cookies: This can be an advertiser attachment from off the Internet into your cookie folder that is on your computer. It can also be attached to spyware to keep track of your every move. They can be positive and harmless to mischievous and annoying some websites won't let you on unless your web browser is cookie enabled. They take up space on your computer clear them as much a possible through computer disk clean up on your computer O/S.

** Phisher: sounds pronounced like fisher spelt like phisher. This is a false sight set-up to look like the real thing. Let's say CiTi Bank. Through e-mail your told the Bank wants you to update your account details. You are then given a link to follow to do so. It looks like the real thing. You are asked to put your information down with credit card then click enters. From that point on they get all your information. And run up bills online with your credit card information. Here's another case scenario off the web:

http://www.channelregister.co.uk

"At this point we have determined that the thieves made approximately 1,100 attempts to steal data with a very

sophisticated strategy that involved
sending staff a total of seven
'phishing' emails, all of which at first
glance appeared legitimate," Thom Mason,
the lab's director, wrote in an email
sent to employees on Monday. "At present
we believe that about 11 staff opened
the attachments, which enabled the
hackers to infiltrate the system and
remove data."

This numbers are staggering as to how
much phishing is going on everyday as I
have stated in the chapter 9111 a great
lashing strike is coming forth in global
terrorism. For a few it is a game for
the new front its wider spread then we
know. And what we do know is only a
small bit of the frosting on the cake.
This attack is all the more the excuse
to bring a new system online before
9111. The elite being the government,
cyber cops those who have the clearances
for whatever agency they might
represent. The more I see this growing
the more I'm almost sure we are heading
for the greatest Internet shut down
ever. Because it is the new unsecured
border into secret systems of the world.
When the shut down comes it will be to
purge the system. You mean every ISP in
the nation will be shutdown at the same
time? Let me say this *Net-Neutrality* means
nothing when it comes to the interest of

the hierarchy, those who are in control of the flow of money. You threaten the security of the money, stocks, bonds, and the stock exchange. You ruffle the feathers of the very officials who run the country from behind the scenes. Before this great build up gets to its worst point there will be a shut down.

I predict it will happen in the springtime or before fall when conditions are right and no one will be to hot or cold. It comes as a brown out at first for some areas or a black out of a whole city.

A lot of your government buildings have back-up power systems that will cover and hospital institutions. The bases will be covered and you'll believe what you want to believe. When this lack of power comes forth as we are already seeing in the Untied States. People conserving water because of shortages and weather changes. This will be the greatest excuse to secretly shut things down and boot up the new system. I've been to places where the power went out but you where able to still pick up the phone and hear a dial tone. Read on some more details I got from this Internet article.

Word of the attacks comes less than a week after security provider McAfee said state-sponsored cyber spying is on the rise, with at least 120 countries using the Internet to conduct espionage. It also comes a few days after MI5, the UK counterintelligence agency, warned UK businesses of the threat posed by state-sponsored Chinese hackers.

You better equip yourself now with a firewall system when you get on line. There are those who are collecting information about you on a daily bases they love to hear people cry about Net-Neutrality like freedom of speech because that gives them power to search out what freedoms you have and who you are and where your located. Things might be moving at a faster pace then what I have thought. But if by 9111 nothing has happened you have one of two things. One they have intercepted the threat before it happens two the agenda has been moved. Then the internet is like one hudge sleeper cell waiting to awake with a rush of denial of service. Either way it will only be a matter of time. This book will be published in 2008 because I've seen a mass of information flood forward as I write the only thing I can do is release the book into the wild as soon as possible. There can always be a follow up book I promise this information will grow it will be covered by New Media as well as regualr networks like usual.
The Hollywood writers guild wants what is their Net-Neutrality like freedom of speech. The right to collect royalites from new media and other sources that for the most part is an information free

highway. In the end I fill they will
have bit off more then what they
bargained for a great loss is coming for
them during these years of Cyber War.
Timing is everything even as I write
this has proven itself true.
**When this was published on the network
it was already obsolete new terms have
popped up even further but this is a
good basic idea of what has been on the
net already. These are the weapons of
the Internet life. Things that can wreck
havoc on your computer. In some cases
the wrong virus or Trojan can shut down
your computer completely. As I said I
couldn't even complete this book in 2007
because the information I've written is
already coming forth before the end of
the year. I haven't covered everything
the information is so vast and keeps
growing. I have Firewalls they slow
things down at times but when I have let
them down its not long afterwards
there's an attack. This is entertainment
in itself sometimes learning to
configure your computer to overcome the
Cyber War on the Net. I use an old
Firewall version and Virus protector
because I know how to update them
manually with appropriate script and
folder exchange. Things like this are
far to advance to learn here in this
book. It's a learning process an
experience I can guarantee increases
intelligence. Even as I have proof

written my book this February 2008 it
has been reported that as many as eight
fiber optic lines for much of the
Internet Mediterranean have been
damaged, even as I have written this at
first it was two now its eight. This
interrupted Internet service to millions
of people in India and Egypt. I believe
it effected Australia as well. This is
the third and most predominate way for
Internet services to be interrupted but
the most noticed if used in an offensive
tactic.

**The Authors additional comments and terms.

The Authors glossary

The New Matrix: is a term I use to
describe a new Internet operating
system that will becoming online
Sometime in the late 21st century.

It will have nothing to do with the
Movie the Matrix but a lot to do with
the old school junk on the Internet
now. It will be an elite system for
those who are in important operations
in the government, economics, and many
other applications toward off the
Enemy within cyber space.

That we have created on the Internet.
It is not the program called Long Horn
it another operating system perhaps
already in use by the government. My
intuition tells me these things and
the visions I have had of the New
World order.

Additional Notes will be added here
for scripts and things dealing with
Virtual world activities. This space
Is reserved for those scripts.

The enemy within: These are the personas we have allowed in every fabric of society on earth in allowing autonomous anonymous handles on the Internet that enemy being ourselves resulting in Transference of those Characters or character into real-time.

Real-time: This is our reality in our everyday lives away from the computer and in the living breathing on planet earth fulfilling or part in society.

Reality Separation: The symptoms are a sudden separation from any present conversation in the real world. The person experiences what is called daydreaming while in real time. They cannot focus on the conversation that is before them because they are dreaming of the cyber world that they have been experiencing for the last 24/7 hours or more.

Godsenders: A fictional term for a group of believers in Christ. They are the light bearers of the information highway. Used in a fictional work by the Author by the same title of the book. They send out the message of Jesus Christ by e-mail and set-up web-sites with the same theme.

Computer Addiction Test

Though these series of questions seem funny at times people have real problems with these issues. These questions are asked everyday within reality base situations with out the computer. In this test we find out how much of the same problems have been transferred to computer and Internet users. You will read the end results of the test at the end this chapter. Therefore I'm in hopes it will help individuals to step away from the computer Internet use to get some serious intervention help before its too late and you are persuaded to carry out actions you'll regret in real-time. In this test rate your response by 1-5 five being the highest response that you agree while 1 is the lowest response that you disagree. The Yes and NO questions I'll explain at the end of this chapter in a reality checking explanation.

Let the Test Begin

This test is subject to change as my studies continue on human behavior and the Internet.

1. Do you feel sorry when you do things wrong? Yes, No

2. After using the computer do you feel depressed more often then not?

   1 2 3 4 5

3. After using the computer do you have bad dreams?

   1 2 3 4 5

4. After using the computer do you have trouble sleeping?

   1 2 3 4 5

5. After using the computer/Internet have you had a loss/gain of appetite?

   1 2 3 4 5

6. Has the computer/Internet ever helped you have thoughts of Suicide?

   1 2 3 4 5

7. Do you have thoughts of homicide after using the Internet?

   1 2 3 4 5

8. Do you think people can read your mind after being in an Internet chat room?

   1 2 3 4 5

9. Do curtain Internet websites put thoughts in your head, or take thoughts out?

   1 2 3 4 5

10. Do you hear voices long after leaving a chat room?

   1 2 3 4 5

11. Do you read between the line things that only you can see?

   1 2 3 4 5

12. Are people spying on you and a part of a major conspiracy?

   1 2 3 4 5

13. Do you feel safe alone with only your computer?

   1 2 3 4 5

14. Do you worry more than most people about Internet news lines?

   1 2 3 4 5

15. Do you easily get angry at reality?

   1 2 3 4 5

16. Do you get along with people when you're away from the computer?

   Yes, No

17. Have you ever have been arrested as a result of a computer crime?

   Yes, No

18. Have you been employed long?

   Yes, No

19. Have you ever been divorced as the result of Internet use?

Yes, No

20.Have you ever been abused?

Yes, No

21.Do you get along with your father?

Yes, No

22.Do you get along with your mother?

Yes, No

23.How was your childhood? Happy or sad, strict or lenient?

To score your self-tally up all your 1-5 answers if your running totals are 14 to 29 chances you have a healthy computer life chances are you are new user and haven't been on more then a year. While 30 to 45 is going in Decline your Internet use has been perhaps five years or more without a lot of alarms going off on your computer use. If there were anything to be concerned about it would be your exploration and experimentation on the Internet. Be alerted when your yes and no questions are negative.

Now, 46 to 60 is good warning that your use of the computer is alarming and it influences you deeply how you think, eat, sleep and socialize. You have been on the computer and the Internet perhaps 5 to 10 years or more. Some of your influences are just starting to create problems with your social life. Anything above 61 to 75 is failing chances are your whole life is influenced by the computer and the Internet you have been on 10 to 12 years or more and have been influenced by the darknet. You could be a hacker a cyber bully, someone who is involved in cyber terrorism. If you are new to the Internet and you think this way I would step away from the Internet and cyber groups. In any case if you score high in the numbers and your not even beginning to enjoy the Internet. You are already approaching an area of concern. The yes and no questions can tell of the issues before you began your use of the computer. Like the last questions from 20 to 22 these can stem from regular issues in your life. Ask yourself have I really addressed these issues before I explore into anyone else's life miles away. I'm not just looking for rebounds from relationship to relationship. It's like the three blind mice you could be leading others astray along with you if the issues aren't fully addressed the issues at hand. Many of chat room conversations start off "Well, I just got a divorce." Or "I was abused child." And everybody relates but come up with no solutions but chitchat on the Internet day by day. Building on top each other the bridge between the real world and cyber life.

Sometimes people will exploit you making you feel they are in the same boat when they are not. Exploiting from money to kidnapping and the like. In essence you create your own limbo and a nowhere land with nowhere plans for nobody I feel safe in front of this little computer screen. You don't really know me so you think while spider ware and other spy wares are collecting information about you from your computer. Be alarmed when you sit in idleness for many hours. Make sure you have a firewall and the best virus software. Just remember someone created it and someone knows the back door to getting through the holes they know how to break it. If there ever was a civil cyber war on the Internet the one that created the program would win they know all the ins and outs and how to shut it down. Science Fiction has a way of being its own self-fulfilling prophecy a lot of what was written in the beginning is happening in reality. Who would of thought man would have set foot on the moon or fly to space looked at universe from far away? So when we think what we can do sometimes it has away of being achieved in reality. Technology is moving so fast to make what appears to be a faster Internet experience to total Internet blur and melt down. We are moving faster then what we can keep up with Wal-Mart puts out the latest software and only a few months later its obsolete.

The software you bought yesterday may not work on your computer with the new software upgrade you get later. I still work with the older machines because I enjoy the experience they bring as at the time they where made. I have three systems right now each on a different level. From my old 586 computer to the Genuine Intel Pentium(r) III Processor Intel MMX(TM) Technology chances are in the near future I'll get Pentium 4 laptop computer and leave it at that with a DSL modem. You have to think about what you need all that for before you buy otherwise you'll never use the full potential it was built for I'd rather have an old system if it's just used to type a letter or create a spread sheet and play simple solitaire games. You don't need anything else its just a simple functional machine. The three computers I have I will use teach about computers to the novice that's all I need. I hope I have made this an interesting read about the computer world and you'll have a better understanding of the future of your personal CPU. Also I hope I have made it interesting read that will help guide you on the Internet with its good points and pitfalls. The questions from 16 to 19

Depending on your answers and the reasons for the answers because as we all know theirs two sides to every story and these deal with variable social issues. These deals with your real life and how you cope with daily situations, again the Internet is not the place to get lost or to run away because like the old saying says " You can't run away from yourself because everywhere you go there you are." Keep it Safe☺

Order out Chaos

In this section we will discuss some
ideas for the beginnings of a Computer
Support groups. Such things as ice
breakers to begin the meetings.
Equal goals of discussions about
Internet fantasy, gambling, porno, and
cyber crimes.
These group meetings are based on tried
and true techniques to help support
group meetings. And to resolve issues in
a group setting. Not recommended for
convicted sex offenders they should be
on a Psychotherapy program. These are
groups formed for intervention and
education.

Support Groups

Consist of a facilitator who operates
with the emphasis of bringing the
collective experiences of its members
around a particular topic in this case
computers and the Internet and its
influence on our daily lives. This is
what is called a PEER group not to be
confused with Psychotherapy groups,
which are run by professionals for the
purpose of psychological support. Also
there are TASK groups which deal with
community issues and policies for common
purposes. EDUCATIONAL groups are for the
purpose of teaching new skills.
BOOK groups get together for the purpose
of reading the latest books or reading

poems. Our PEER group is focused on one common theme about Computers and the Internet and many things associated with its use as a user. Processes of open sharing about our thoughts, feelings and experiences between members who have lived for the computer. Each member's goal is to find the common ground for the usefulness of the computer age and its downfalls into introverted social life. Provide honest feedback as to its influence on our lives or strongholds. The dynamic is that each member can return to the group meetings each week or as its designated to share their experiences and any concepts incorporated in the computer world. Helping to educated each other about the computer and the Internet. It is not a shame-based group our goals are not for fostering any negative aspect of the Internet and computer. Its to help educate each other how live a safe and social life with other people who have had the same habits.

It wouldn't hurt Internet corporations like E-Harmony and the like to invest into social peer group awareness. A safety buffer zone in each major city for groups to meet paired couples who have met on the Internet. You have to start the reality relationship. Also it might help screen potential predators who are hunting on the Internet.

In the Beginning.

Everyone leaves all electronic devices at the door in their car wherever. No cell phones, blue tooth's, iphones ipods, laptops, and alarmed watches aren't to be brought into the sacred space. For lack of term here I use this term as in the tradition renderings of a name. Native Americans had Sacred Mountains and spaces, as do other spiritual circles.

There must be respect to each other with tolerance to their beliefs agree to disagree; that's not the purpose here to explore each other's religion or belief system. The groups are formed to loosen those things that bind us from our everyday routines. Quiet music is played while people are entering into the meeting just soft music with no convictions just an atmosphere of ease.

Nothing with lyrics or loud music you must create a soothing atmosphere. The environment must be one free from 24/7 work alcoholic atmosphere or conversation. Perhaps silent prayer, or meditation of some sorts to free the mind and create a Spiritual Space. Some may say this space is humanistic others spiritual.

The achievement here is focus of those
things that cause us to have a lot of
mind chatter. Preferably sit on the
floor the way you feel the most
comfortable. But always have chairs
present for people who prefer to sit
this is good for people who are new to
the meetings. Try to arrange things in
such away everyone is comfortable the
way they are seated. This is not an A.A.
N.A. or A.V. meeting where you sit in a
circle to confess to each other. This is
a place to reduce the everyday 24/7 work
a day atmosphere. In fact you are trying
to forget about work and electronic
devices of every type. The first half
hour is devoted to being still if music
helps to achieve this then keep the
music flowing if total silence help then
shut the music off by mutual agreement.

We are creating individual spaces as
much as possible during the whole first
hour. After that comes open door
discussion.

Naming your Group

Obviously PEER group is a boring name so pick a name that reflects the groups purpose. Computer Anonymous sounds too much like AA find something unique that doesn't create a shame base atmosphere something all can connect to don't make it sound like a bible study either that's not the purpose. If you call it anything to do with the word Cell it sounds like a terrorist group or a religious group. It doesn't mean that only computer geeks or hacks are welcome at these meetings. It really is important for people who need a peace of mind to come to these meetings. People with many worries and weights upon their shoulders. That's the purpose is to create peace of mind from disgruntled atmospheres.

Now the conversations will be work related what we can do to bring to peace of mind to our everyday lives to break routine.

Including inner connecting with family and friends. Finding out what we have lost when we loose ourselves in our moneymaker jobs. Explore an entrepreneur that's its OK to work for you and not relying on others to provide for the job. Explore the good sides of having a boss what good points you have all around. Try to get to the depth of why you disconnect at your work or on the computer. What alienates you from your job, family, and others or visa versa. So many topics to choose from based on environment and atmosphere we are creating around us. Deal with unemployment again this isn't shame based nor do we act like nags to get our point across about unemployment. In fact these are the issues you are looking for when the human dynamic becomes egotistic.

We are looking to calm our over achievements by pulling back on the reigns to relax.

The charismatic character must learn to relax; sometimes these are the ones who run full force and never look in the mirror at them selves. Everything is fast playing with no pause maybe a 15 minute lunch break. Today the 40-hour workweek is dissolving and 80 hours and more fuel the well-oiled machines until you loose out on realities. Lots of people don't take vacations but collect the check and continue to work. Conduct field trips take your group to the park, to art museums or classic music sit by the water falls and listen to the stream and nature alone Maybe a camp retreat of some type to break away.

Advertising

To get this new group going you need to advertise in your local papers sometimes you can get free advertising. Put posters up in your local library, bookstores, and community bulletin boards. Tell them what about the focus group you're starting. Each group can have its individual unique focus it can be Spiritual dealing with faith, or it can be more Physiological focus group perhaps with professional help. In all education and learning from one another pulling the extreme introvert out of their box. Calming the over achiever Down getting the work alcoholic to relax enjoy the goodness of life and nature in itself.

While I had a lot more to add to this chapter I can only conclude here. Let me say this I'm working on a help manual for these exercises to work. Also I running test groups in areas where I live and in other communities. If you are interested in these Focus Peer groups please write or email me for your input. We can start your group were you are living at right now. I'll need volunteers to find areas of interest to help the focus grow.

And to help write Facilitator materials to help instruct and teach all generations involved in this new technology.

Focus Groups
P.O.Box 323
Harlowton, Mt. 59036

Write me for seminors In your area, book
reviews or group discusions.
Consulations for Work place awareness,
schools, or religious meetings for
concerned citizens,and Law enforcement,
or government security. I show several
protective programs you can install on
your computer to protect yourself and
your children against internet predators
and cyber bullies. Also dealing with
security issues for business employee
monitoring. I can recommend Security
Software and hardware to protect you and
your family.
Charges in travel time and materials may
apply in US and Canada, please write me
for that information or e-mail me. TY
e-mail : isentry@netzero.com
www.montanacollections.com

Appendix

1.   Patti Testerman is content manager at JournalGenie.com

2.   Kevin L. Poulsen is editorial director of SecurityFocus.com.

3.   01/28/2006 Art Bell interview with Bot Masters,

4.   Understanding People by J Omar Brubaker, M.A., Robert E. Clark, Ed. D. 1984 Second edition

5.   The Future Shock, The Movie and Book is paradox to the 21st century.

6.   To Catch a Predator part 3, MSNBC Date Line 02/04/06 they have a large series of these programs now. I'm afraid the mind has been burnt like a hot iron they have crossed the barrier of no return. The games of the Internet have convinced them they can go further and bring it into the real world. The self-esteem is deceived into this god syndrome. The master of the domain gets caught up into reality, real-time when he/she finds out they've been tricked.

I suggest that the record should reflect for their characters before judgment and that they go into recovery treatment. If they aren't repeated offenders they need treatment not behind the bars of in sensitive jail.

This doesn't address the mental reprogramming that needs to go on. The net has many strong personalities, teachers of deceptions.

You need to know the history of whom if any they have learned this behavior from. And what got them started on this path in the first place. Internet recovery is important before you destroy people's lives on public Television you must discover what triggered it in the first place the Internet is a mesmerizing tool. Its influence is worldwide I don't recommend it for the weak minded.

7. NIV Bible

8. The New Jerusalem Bible (1985)

9. Aol News: article sources

10. The Age: article sources

11. Sfgate.com: article sources.

12. Geek.com & Reuters, article sources.

13. Carlton Sheets "No money down."

14. "The Day the Dollar Dies." Willard Cantelon in the Christian world. 1981 I do believe that some of what Willard said has come to past some twenty years

later. He was my Pastors brother Pastor
Paul Cantelon I remember sitting through
many meetings of Willard's speaking
engagements. While many words can
empress us we must look at the raw data
and see how far most of the information
comes. I'd say good 45% of this book has
appeared to come true in our present
times. While some figures I remember
seem like it was happening in the
percent of 1980 it was indeed far off to
another time, I remember images of the
cold war but this wasn't the end-time
scenario the extremist where looking for
the end to come and Christ to appear.
15. "When Your Money Fails: The "666
System" is here by Mary Stewart Relfe.
1981 this book has inspired a lot of
paranoia over the number 6 people
including the author was seeing 6 into
everything. Willard Cantelon endorsed
this book.
16. Cell Church Magazine by M.Scott
Boren.

17: Humanity's Team Study group, by Rose
Wolfenbarger.

18:Dec/7/2007
http://www.channelregister.co.uk/2007/12
/07/national_labs_breached/
19. http://www3.ca.com/virusinfo

Virus updates

When you're done with this book read:

I'm a very special book. You see. I'm traveling around the world making friends. I hope I've made another one in you. If so, please go to www.bookcrossing.com, where you can make a brief journal entry with my BCID number 343-5839163. You will see where I've been, and my old friends will be happy to know I'm safe here in your hands. Then keep my dream alive-read & releases me!

BCID: 343-5839163

First Released by: Ghostwriter Extreme Other volumes might appear somewhere in the world from geocaching.com

Journal

Journal

Journal

Journal

Journal

Journal

Journal

www.ingramcontent.com/pod-product-compliance
Lightning Source LLC
Chambersburg PA
CBHW071225050326
40689CB00011B/2468